CHECKERBOARD BIOGRAPHY LIBRARY

EXPLORERS

Jacques Cartier

Kristin Petrie

ABDO
Publishing Company

visit us at
www.abdopub.com

Published by ABDO Publishing Company, 4940 Viking Drive, Edina, Minnesota 55435. Copyright © 2004 by Abdo Consulting Group, Inc. International copyrights reserved in all countries. No part of this book may be reproduced in any form without written permission from the publisher.

Printed in the United States.

Cover Photos: Corbis, North Wind
Interior Photos: Corbis pp. 5, 6, 7, 8, 9, 11, 15, 18, 21, 23, 25, 27, 28, 29; North Wind pp. 17, 19, 24

Series Coordinator: Stephanie Hedlund
Editors: Kate A. Conley, Kristin Van Cleaf
Art Direction & Cover Design: Neil Klinepier
Interior Design & Maps: Dave Bullen

Library of Congress Cataloging-in-Publication Data

Petrie, Kristin, 1970-
    Jacques Cartier / Kristin Petrie.
        p. cm. -- (Explorers)
    Summary: Brief text describes the life and travels of the sixteenth-century French navigator who made three voyages to what is today known as Canada, in search of a northwest passage to China.
    Includes bibliographical references and index.
    ISBN 1-59197-594-8
    1. Cartier, Jacques, 1491-1557--Juvenile literature. 2. Explorers--America--Biography--Juvenile literature. 3. Explorers--France--Biography--Juvenile literature. 4. America--Discovery and exploration--French--Juvenile literature. 5. Canada--History--To 1763 (New France)--Juvenile literature. [1. Cartier, Jacques, 1491-1557. 2. Explorers. 3. Canada--Discovery and exploration. 4. Canada--History--To 1763 (New France)] I. Title.

E133.C3P48 2004
971.01'13'092--dc22
[B]   2003066546

Contents

Jacques Cartier

The 1400s and 1500s were a time of exploration. Explorers around the world were taking to the water. What lay across the Atlantic Ocean? What riches were to be found? These were the questions on everyone's mind.

Jacques Cartier asked these questions, too. Back in the 1500s, this Frenchman searched for a northern sea route to China. Explorers called this fabled route the **Northwest Passage**. On Cartier's search, he discovered Canada.

Cartier became the first European to map this new land. He also attempted to establish a settlement there. Cartier's discovery was the basis for France's claim to this land. Join us, as we explore Canada's St. Lawrence area with Jacques Cartier.

1451
Christopher Columbus born

1485
Hernán Cortés born

1450
John Cabot born

1460
Vasco da Gama born

1491
Jacques Cartier born

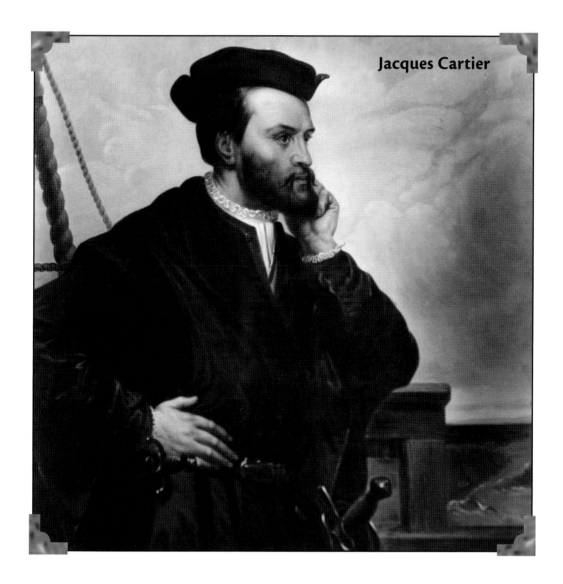

Jacques Cartier

1492
Columbus's first voyage west for Spain

1496
Cabot's first voyage for England

1493
Columbus's second voyage, attempted to colonize Hispaniola

Before Canada

Jacques Cartier was born in 1491 in Saint-Malo, France. Most harbors in Europe had ships coming from and going on exploratory voyages. The port of Saint-Malo was no exception. Like all young children, Jacques was probably influenced by the excitement and activity in the port.

Not much is known of Jacques's early life. There is no record of his schooling. Some historians believe, however, that he studied navigation in the city of Dieppe, a French center for navigators.

Saint-Malo in the 1600s

1497
Cabot's second voyage, discovered the Grand Banks; da Gama was first to sail around Africa to India

1496 or 1497
Hernando de Soto born

1498
Cabot's third voyage, may have died; Columbus's third voyage

Some scholars believe Jacques made several trips across the Atlantic Ocean as a young man. He may have been on a fishing **fleet** to the Grand Banks of Newfoundland. He may also have visited Brazil.

In 1520, Jacques married Catherine des Granches. Four years later, he is believed to have sailed with Italian navigator Giovanni da Verrazano to the North American coast. Verrazano sailed from the coast of North Carolina to Newfoundland. He proved that North America was a huge continent.

Giovanni da Verrazano

1502
Columbus's fourth voyage; da Gama's second voyage

1506
Columbus died

1504
Cortés sailed to the West Indies

First Voyage

In 1534, King Francis I of France hired Cartier to explore the possibility of a passage to Asia. He encouraged Cartier to claim land for France and discover countries with gold and other valuables.

Cartier's first voyage began on April 20, 1534. He sailed from Saint-Malo with two ships and a small crew of 61 men. It took just 20 days to reach Cape Bonavista, Newfoundland.

From Cape Bonavista, Cartier sailed north. At the tip of Newfoundland, the ships turned south and sailed between Newfoundland and Labrador. It was here that Jacques Cartier made his first important discovery. This waterway, named the Strait of Belle Isle, led to a gulf.

Cartier and his crew watch for land.

1511
Cortés helped take over Cuba

1510
Francisco Vásquez de Coronado born

1514
De Soto went to the New World

The ships crossed the gulf to Prince Edward Island and the Magdalen Islands. Cartier thought they were part of the mainland of Asia. He didn't know they were islands! When he reached Gaspé **Peninsula**, he claimed it for France.

While exploring this region, Cartier met the area's natives. The **Micmac** were friendly and eager to trade. The French and Micmac celebrated their meeting. Then, they began exchanging furs for iron knives and hatchets.

Another of Cartier's goals was to bring Christianity to the natives.

The French were also friendly with the Iroquois, another Native American tribe from the region. The Iroquois told Cartier of precious jewels, metals, and wealthy kingdoms farther to the northwest. They watched closely while the French put up a wooden cross as a landmark.

Cartier visited with Iroquois chief Donnacona. The chief was then convinced to allow his two sons to journey to France. The boys would learn French and become interpreters for Cartier. Some historians believe that Cartier kidnapped the boys.

Cartier and his crew returned to their ships on July 25. They sailed farther north, exploring the island of Anticosti. At the western end of Anticosti Island, Cartier noted the mouth of a large river. However, the crew decided strong winds made sailing on too dangerous.

Cartier led his ships back to the Strait of Belle Isle and the open Atlantic. On September 5, 1534, they reached Saint-Malo. The voyage had lasted 15 weeks.

1524
Da Gama's third voyage, died in Cochin, India

1519–1521
Cortés conquered the Aztec Empire and claimed Mexico for Spain

1532
De Soto helped attack the Inca Empire

Would you turn back if you discovered a river that you thought could take you to Asia? How do you think the crew convinced Cartier to head home?

Cartier and crew raise a cross as a landmark.

W. Croome.

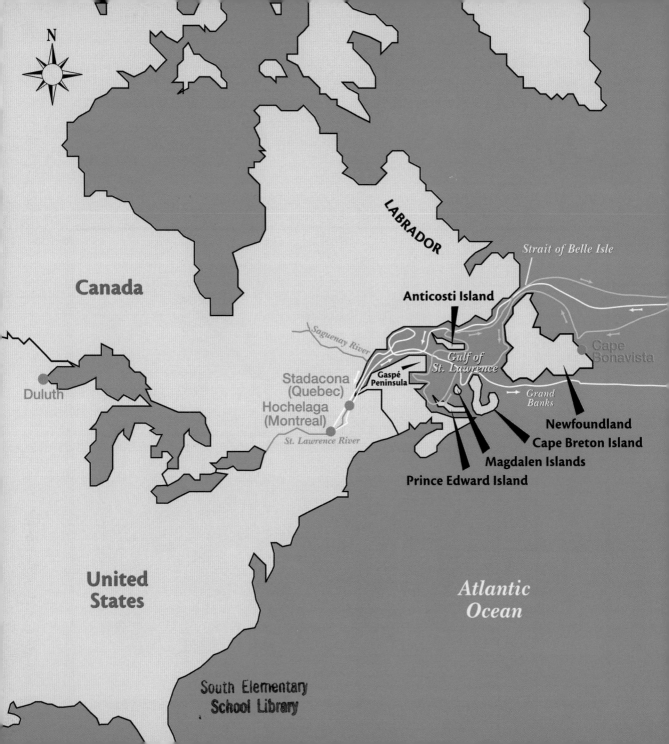

N

LABRADOR

Strait of Belle Isle

Canada

Anticosti Island

Saguenay River

Gulf of
St. Lawrence

Cape
Bonavista

Stadacona
(Quebec)

Gaspé
Peninsula

Duluth

Hochelaga
(Montreal)

St. Lawrence River

Grand
Banks

Newfoundland

Cape Breton Island

Magdalen Islands

Prince Edward Island

United
States

Atlantic
Ocean

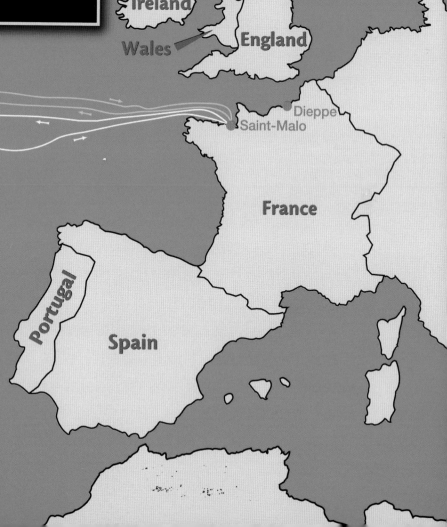

The Journeys of Jacques Cartier

——→	1534
——→	1535 AND 1541

Northern Ireland

Scotland

Ireland

Wales

England

Dieppe

Saint-Malo

France

Atlantic Ocean

Portugal

Spain

Second Voyage

Cartier returned to France with two Native Americans and the first corn seen in Europe. He told of a possible **Northwest Passage** to the west of Newfoundland.

The explorer also shared the stories of wealthy nations that were reported to be along the route. It's no wonder the king of France immediately granted Cartier a second voyage.

Cartier set sail from Saint-Malo again on May 19, 1535. His **fleet** included three ships, with 110 men and the two Native American boys.

After crossing the Atlantic, Cartier sailed through the Strait of Belle Isle again. This time, however, he sailed along the coast of Labrador.

On August 10, Cartier reached the northern point of Gaspé **Peninsula**. The fleet entered a bay and named it St. Lawrence, because it was that saint's **feast day**. Moving on,

1534
Cartier's first voyage for France

1539–1542
De Soto explored La Florida

1533
De Soto helped take over Cuzco

1535
Cartier's second voyage

he noted the large mouth of a river. It was also named for Saint Lawrence.

With the help of the Iroquois boys, the expedition continued its journey west on the river. The crew reached a Native American village called Stadacona, which is now known as Quebec. Donnacona greeted Cartier. But for unknown reasons, Donnacona didn't want him to sail farther west.

The St. Lawrence River today

Cartier left the boys behind and continued his exploration upriver. Next the group reached Hochelaga, another Native American village. It is now Montreal. Cartier climbed a mountain at the edge of this village and named it *Mont Réal*, meaning "Mount Royal."

From the mountain, Cartier could see **rapids** to the west on the St. Lawrence River. He named them *La Chine Rapids*, meaning the "China Rapids." He thought that China lay just beyond them.

By this time in the expedition it was winter. The Frenchmen were not used to the very cold temperatures. So, Cartier decided to turn back.

The crew spent the winter in a fort they had built at Stadacona. Twenty-five of the crew members died from **scurvy**. A brew made from white cedar, which contained vitamin C, saved the rest of the crew's lives.

During their stay, the **Huron** shared tales about a wealthy kingdom to the north. They called it Saguenay, and

Would You?

Would you try to scare Cartier away? Donnacona's tribe dressed as ghosts to scare the Frenchmen. How would you try to get them to leave?

1547
Cortés died

1557
Cartier died

1542
Coronado returned to New Spain; de Soto died

1554
Coronado died

1566
Drake's first voyage to the New World

they said it was full of gold and other treasures. Unfortunately, the Frenchmen didn't understand that the **Huron** only told the stories for amusement.

Cartier was eager to report to King Francis I about the riches in the stories. When spring arrived, Cartier sailed back to France. Among Cartier's passengers were the Iroquois chief Donnacona and some members of his tribe. They landed in Saint-Malo on July 16, 1536.

On this second voyage, Cartier had proved that Newfoundland was an island. He had also uncovered the St. Lawrence River as an entry point to an unknown continent. He still hoped this continent would provide a passage to China.

King Francis I of France

1567
Drake's second voyage

1577
Drake began a worldwide voyage, was first Englishman to sail the Pacific Ocean

1570 and 1572
Drake terrorized the Spanish in the New World

Canada is from the Huron-Iroquois word *kanata*. It means "village" or "settlement." Cartier used the word for the first settlement around Quebec, which he could see from Mont Reál (*right*). Later, *Canada* referred to New France.

Third Voyage

Cartier was eager to make a third expedition. He wanted to search for Saguenay and the riches the **Huron** had talked about. Chief Donnacona fueled the excitement.

Once Donnacona realized how much the Europeans prized gold and jewels, he **embellished** his stories. He swore there were many riches in Canada and Saguenay. Cartier was eager to look for these riches. But a war between France and Spain **postponed** the voyage for five years.

The third journey was much different from Cartier's earlier voyages. The expedition included several ships and 1,000 people, most of whom were convicts. This voyage was for more than exploring. The French aimed to colonize the new land.

For this reason, the king commissioned Jean-François de La Rocque de Roberval to command the expedition. The nobleman was named lieutenant general of the North American territory.

1588
Drake helped England win the Battle of Gravelines against Spain's Invincible Armada

Roberval took a long time to prepare for his voyage. He had to organize an army and all of its **ammunition**. Cartier was in command of five ships. He was ready before Roberval. So, Cartier left the port of Saint-Malo on May 23, 1541, without the lieutenant general.

Jacques Cartier

Would you have believed the stories Donnacona told? Make up your own story about the riches of Canada.

1728
James Cook born

1765
Boone journeyed to Florida

1768
Cook sailed for Tahiti

1734
Daniel Boone born

1767
Boone explored Kentucky

Cartier waited three months at Newfoundland for Roberval. When he did not arrive, Cartier sailed on to Canada. The **fleet** made its way up the St. Lawrence River to Stadacona.

Cartier searched for a good site for his colony. He chose a point near the Rouge River, west of Quebec. This site had good land for farming and trees for fuel and building.

The settlers built a fort called Cap Rouge and prepared for winter. While this was going on, the crew was looking for the promised treasures. They were rewarded with the discovery of gold and diamonds.

Cartier decided to search for Saguenay and its treasures on his own. He explored the St. Lawrence River until it was no longer navigable by his ships. After reaching Hochelaga, the discouraged explorer turned back to his fort for the winter.

The following months were difficult. Natives in the region became hostile after they realized the French intended to

Quebec has grown since Cartier's time. In 2003, more than 167,000 people lived there.

1778
Cook became the first European to record Hawaiian Islands; Boone captured by Shawnee

1775
Boone cut the Wilderness Road from Virginia to Kentucky

1779
Cook died

This map shows Hochelaga and Saguenay as Cartier may have seen it.

stay. Many of the French were sick with **scurvy**. In addition, Roberval had not arrived with supplies for the colony.

Roberval still had not arrived by the spring of 1542. So, Cartier started his return voyage to France. He found Roberval and his **fleet** in Newfoundland.

Roberval ordered Cartier to return to the settlement in Canada, but Cartier refused. He continued on his way back to France with his shipload of gold and diamonds.

Back in Saint-Malo, Cartier learned that the large quantity of diamonds and gold were really quartz and pyrite. Both treasures were nearly worthless!

1813
John C. Frémont born

1842
Frémont's first independent surveying mission

1820
Boone died

Would you disobey Roberval's order and return to France? What do you think were Cartier's reasons for returning to France?

Pyrite is an iron mineral. But its gold color often fools people into thinking it is the precious metal. So, pyrite is often called fool's gold.

Quartz is very important in today's economy. It is used in jewelry, ceramics, and glass. However, it was not always as widely used.

Cartier's Legacy

Cartier spent the rest of his life near Saint-Malo. He died on September 1, 1557. He probably still wondered whether the St. Lawrence River led to China.

Cartier did not find the riches he sought. He didn't uncover the **Northwest Passage**. And, his attempt to colonize Canada failed.

However, Cartier accomplished many great things. He discovered new waterways. He explored new lands. He met new nations of people and set up trade with them. He also sailed farther into the New World than explorers had before him.

Cartier's documentation of these expeditions was the best of his time. Fifty years after his death, the explorer's detailed notes helped the French successfully settle Canada.

1856
Frémont ran for president of the United States but lost

1845-1846
Frémont explored the Great Basin and the Pacific Coast, fought in the Mexican War

1890
Frémont died

This statue of Cartier is in Saint-Malo, where he was born.

1910
Jacques Cousteau born

1951
Cousteau's first expedition in the Red Sea

1942
Cousteau and Gagnan developed the Aqua-Lung for diving

Montreal, Canada

In 1608, Frenchman Samuel de Champlain founded the city of Quebec on the site of Cartier's settlement. The city of Montreal, founded in 1642, was named for the nearby mountain that Cartier had named Mont Réal. For nearly 150 years, Canada was known as New France.

The British took over Canada in 1759. But, this change in power did not end the French influence that Jacques Cartier had established. French traditions and **culture** continue to this day.

The French spirit of navigation also continues. In 1959, the waterways from Cartier's La Chine **Rapids** to the Great Lakes were connected. Using a series of canals and **locks**, ships can now travel from the Atlantic Ocean all the way to Duluth, Minnesota.

Since 1959, ships have been able to sail 2,342 miles (3,770 km) from the Atlantic Ocean to Duluth, Minnesota. There, they sail under the aerial lift bridge to enter the port of Duluth.

Glossary

ammunition - bullets, shells, and other items used in firearms.

culture - the customs, arts, and tools of a nation or people at a certain time.

embellish - to make something more attractive by adding details that may not be true.

feast day - a religious ceremony and feast to celebrate a saint.

fleet - a group of ships under one command.

Huron - a Native American of an Iroquoian tribe formerly living between Lake Huron and Lake Ontario.

lock - on a river, a closed space with gates on each end. It is used to raise or lower boats to different water levels along the river.

Micmac - a Native American of an Algonquian tribe living in the maritime provinces of Canada.

Northwest Passage - a passage by sea between the Pacific and Atlantic oceans along the north coast of North America.

peninsula - land that sticks out into water and is connected to a larger landmass.

postponed - put off until a later time.

rapid - a fast-moving part of a river. Rocks or logs often break the surface of the water in this area.

scurvy - a fatal disease caused by a lack of vitamin C.

Saying It

Dieppe - DYEHP
Gaspé Peninsula - ga-SPAY puh-NIHNT-suh-luh
Hochelaga - hah-shuh-LA-guh
Jacques Cartier - zhahk kar-tyay
Jean-François de La Rocque de Roberval - zhahn-frahn-swah
duh la rawk duh raw-behr-val
Labrador - LA-bruh-dawr
Magdalen Islands - MAG-duh-luhn EYE-luhnds
Saguenay - sa-guh-NAY

Web Sites

To learn more about Jacques Cartier, visit ABDO Publishing
Company on the World Wide Web at **www.abdopub.com**.
Web sites about Jacques Cartier are featured on our Book Links
page. These links are routinely monitored and updated to
provide the most current information available.

Index